MARRAKECH TRAVEL GUIDE 2024 UPDATED

Your Ultimate Guide to the Marvels and Mysteries of Morocco's Jewel City

Max Sterling

MARRAKESH PRACTICAL TIPS AND ADVICE

CONCLUSION

WELCOME TO MARRAKESH

Welcome to Marrakesh, a city that beckons with the allure of a thousand tales woven into the fabric of its vibrant streets and bustling souks. Have you ever wondered how Marrakesh earned its nickname, "The Red City," inspired by the terracotta-hued walls that seem to embrace centuries of history under the Moroccan sun?

Beyond its iconic red walls lies a metropolis that has stood witness to centuries of Berber, Arab, and

French influences, creating a unique blend of tradition and modernity. The medina, a UNESCO World Heritage Site, serves as the beating heart of Marrakesh, where each step leads to a discovery – be it a hidden riad adorned with intricate tiles, a spice-scented market stall, or a tranquil courtyard where the soothing sounds of a fountain offer respite from the bustling streets.

One of Marrakesh's unique features is Jardin Majorelle, a botanical oasis that was once the private retreat of French painter Jacques Majorelle. The garden, a mesmerizing canvas of cobalt blue buildings, lush greenery, and vibrant plant life, is now open to the public. It stands as a testament to the city's ability to embrace creativity and provide an escape into a realm of natural beauty amidst the vibrant chaos.

As you traverse the city, the Koutoubia Mosque's towering minaret acts as a steadfast guide, offering a sense of direction in the maze-like alleys. The call to prayer resonates through the air, creating a harmonious backdrop to the city's dynamic rhythm.

HISTORY OF MARRAKESH

Founded in 1062 by Youssef bin Tachfine, Marrakesh has a deep and rich history that has shaped its unique identity. As the seat of the Almoravid Empire, it quickly became a thriving center for trade and cultural exchange. The city's strategic location in the foothills of the Atlas Mountains and its proximity to the Sahara Desert facilitated trade along trans-Saharan routes, making it a melting pot of Berber, Arab, and African influences.

The Almoravids constructed the Koutoubia Mosque in the 12th century, an architectural masterpiece that would set the tone for the city's future developments. Under the Almohads in the 12th and 13th centuries, Marrakesh continued to flourish, witnessing the construction of impressive structures like the Kasbah and the Menara Gardens.

In the 16th century, the Saadian dynasty left its mark with the construction of the Saadian Tombs and the El Badi Palace. These structures showcased the city's opulence and the Saadian rulers' patronage of the arts and architecture.

Marrakesh has been a cultural and intellectual hub for centuries. The Ben Youssef Madrasa, built during the Merinid dynasty in the 14th century, became one of the most important Islamic schools in North Africa. It attracted scholars and students from various parts of the Muslim world.

The 20th century brought significant changes to Marrakesh with the arrival of the French. While the city maintained its cultural and spiritual significance, the French Protectorate led to the development of the Ville Nouvelle, a new European-influenced district. The juxtaposition of the ancient medina and the modern Ville Nouvelle adds to the city's diverse character.

After gaining independence in 1956, Morocco, and by extension Marrakesh, experienced a renewed sense of national identity and pride. Tourism became a pivotal industry, drawing visitors to the city's historic sites, vibrant markets, and enchanting gardens.

Today, Marrakesh stands as a testament to its enduring history. The medina's narrow winding streets house ancient palaces, mosques, and bustling souks. Jardin Majorelle, created by French painter Jacques Majorelle and later owned by Yves Saint Laurent, showcases a fusion of Moroccan and French influences. The Djemaa el-Fna square pulsates with life, offering a vibrant snapshot of Marrakesh's cultural richness.

DISTRICTS AND NEIGHBORHOODS

Dive into the kaleidoscope of Marrakesh's districts and neighborhoods, where each corner tells a story waiting to be uncovered. From the bustling energy of the medina to the chic allure of Gueliz, every district is a chapter in the city's vibrant narrative.

Medina

Welcome to the heart and soul of Marrakesh – the Medina. This ancient city center is a labyrinth of narrow alleys, hidden riads, and bustling souks that transport you back in time. Imagine getting lost in the vibrant chaos of Jemaa el-Fna, where snake charmers, storytellers, and vibrant market stalls create an electrifying atmosphere. The Medina is a treasure trove of historic landmarks like the Koutoubia Mosque, Saadian Tombs, and the Bahia Palace, each telling tales of Marrakesh's rich past. As you wander through its maze, let the centuries-old architecture and the aromatic scents of spices guide you through this living museum.

What to do and see

Start your day at Jemaa el-Fna Square. It's a buzzing market by day – picture stalls filled with colorful spices, artisans crafting unique treasures, and the air filled with the sounds of snake charmers and storytellers. As the sun sets, the square transforms into a magical carnival of lights, music, and irresistible street food. Join in the festivities, let the rhythm of the drums guide your steps, and savor the flavors of Morocco.

Next up, the Koutoubia Mosque. You can't miss its towering minaret, a landmark that defines Marrakesh's skyline. Wander around the peaceful gardens, where the fragrance of orange blossoms fills the air. Capture the play of sunlight on the intricate patterns of the minaret – it's a photographer's dream.

Now, venture into the hidden gem of Saadian Tombs. Tucked away behind ancient walls, this burial site unveils a serene courtyard adorned with historic tombs. Imagine the stories etched into these walls, tales of Marrakesh's royal past waiting to be discovered.

Continue your journey to Bahia Palace, a feast for the eyes with its elaborate architecture and lush gardens. Get lost in the hidden corners, where fragrant orange trees and vibrant flowers create a haven of tranquility. It's like stumbling upon a secret garden within the bustling Medina.

Don't forget the Souks – the beating heart of Marrakesh's commerce. Lose yourself in the narrow alleys filled with treasures. Bargain with local artisans, shop for spices, textiles, and leather goods. Let each purchase be a piece of the Medina to take home with you.

Ben Youssef Madrasa is your next stop, an intellectual oasis within the chaos. Explore the courtyards and study rooms, where the echoes of ancient scholars linger. Take a moment in the peaceful surroundings for quiet contemplation.

Dive into the cultural richness of Marrakesh by visiting Dar Si Said Museum. It's a haven for traditional artifacts and crafts, offering a deeper understanding of Morocco's artistic heritage. Then, transport yourself through time at Maison de la Photographie, where vintage photographs tell the captivating story of the country's history.

Explore the ruins of El Badi Palace, an open-air museum of grandeur turned to remnants. Climb to the top for panoramic views of Marrakesh and the Atlas Mountains – a scene that will be etched in your memory.

End your journey at Dar El Bacha, a cultural convergence where history meets contemporary art. Attend live performances, immerse yourself in art exhibitions, and soak in the dynamic cultural scene that thrives within the Medina.

Finally, wander through El Mellah, the historic Jewish Quarter. Feel the diversity as you explore synagogues, markets, and alleys. Don't miss the chance to indulge in Jewish-Moroccan cuisine, a fusion of flavors that mirrors the cultural tapestry of Marrakesh.

Gueliz

In stark contrast to the ancient charm of the Medina, Gueliz is Marrakesh's modern heartbeat. Here, wide boulevards, contemporary boutiques, and stylish cafes create a cosmopolitan ambiance. Picture yourself strolling along Avenue Mohammed V, lined with fashion-forward shops and art galleries. Gueliz is where tradition meets trendiness, offering a dynamic blend of Moroccan culture and European influences. As night falls, the district comes alive with trendy bars and restaurants, providing a chic escape from the historical allure of the Medina.

What to do and see

Start your journey at the Majorelle Garden, a place that's like a green oasis in the heart of the city. Picture yourself strolling through vibrant blue pathways, surrounded by exotic plants, and soaking in the tranquility. And guess what? Right next door is the Yves Saint Laurent Museum, a haven for fashion enthusiasts. Explore the exhibits, relive the glamour of haute couture, and maybe even strike a pose in front of the iconic architecture.

Now, let's talk cafes. Gueliz is a haven for coffee lovers and those who appreciate a good ambiance. Imagine yourself at Café de la Poste, sipping on your favorite brew and watching the world go by. Or, for a dose of artistic vibes, head to Café des Épices, where every cup feels like a masterpiece.

But wait, there's more! Gueliz is not just about gardens and coffee; it's a canvas for street art. Take a leisurely stroll through the alleys, admire the vibrant murals, and let the urban art scene tell its own story. You might stumble upon a hidden gem or two, adding a touch of creativity to your day.

And then comes shopping. Carre Eden is like a retail therapy haven, offering everything from international brands to local treasures. Imagine yourself as a fashionista, exploring the diverse boutiques and curating your own style from this eclectic shopping center.

As the sun sets, Gueliz transforms into a nightlife hotspot. From rooftop bars with stunning views to lively nightclubs that keep the party going, envision yourself as the life of the Gueliz nightlife scene. Dance, laugh, and make memories against the backdrop of the city lights.

Now, let's talk food. Gueliz is a culinary delight with restaurants that cater to every palate. Whether you're indulging in gourmet experiences at Le Comptoir du Pacha or savoring local flavors at La Famille, see yourself as a culinary explorer, discovering the diverse tastes that Gueliz has to offer.

But Gueliz isn't just about indulgence; it's about relaxation too. Pamper yourself at one of the luxurious hammams or spas. Envision each spa session as a chapter in your relaxation diary, allowing Gueliz to soothe both your body and soul.

And finally, blend in with the local elegance. Gueliz is a trendsetter in fashion, so experiment with your attire. Picture yourself as a fashion-forward explorer, capturing the essence of modern Moroccan style.

Hivernage

For those seeking luxury and refinement, Hivernage is a sophisticated oasis within Marrakesh. This upscale district boasts opulent hotels, exclusive spas, and gourmet restaurants. Imagine lounging by a shimmering pool surrounded by lush gardens or savoring a Michelin-starred meal under the starlit sky. Hivernage is synonymous with elegance and tranquility, offering a retreat from the bustling energy of the Medina. It's a haven where the city's elite and discerning travelers indulge in the finer things Marrakesh has to offer.

What to do and see

Picture yourself at the Royal Theatre, a cultural haven where performances from around the world grace the stage. It's not just a venue; it's a gateway to artistic exploration. Check the schedule, and you might find yourself immersed in the drama of a Broadway-worthy show or the rhythmic beats of an international concert.

Now, meander through Marrakesh Plaza, a shopping haven that feels like a luxurious dream. High-end boutiques beckon, surrounded by modern architecture and the scent of freshly brewed coffee. Treat yourself to a shopping spree or simply bask in the ambiance, appreciating the blend of opulence and greenery.

As you continue your journey, the Four Seasons Resort stands like a palace amidst gardens, offering a retreat into tranquility. Even if you're not checking in, consider dining at one of its renowned restaurants or indulging in a spa treatment – it's a taste of paradise in the heart of Hivernage.

Hivernage Square, with its gastronomic delights, is a feast for the senses. Imagine an evening spent dining al fresco, the ambient lighting casting a warm glow over your culinary adventure. The square becomes a lively hub where flavors from around the world converge.

Pass by the Palais des Congrès, a modern architectural marvel that reflects Marrakesh's global appeal. Check for any conferences or events – you might stumble upon an intellectual gathering or a cultural happening that adds unexpected charm to your visit.

For art enthusiasts, the Hivernage Art Gallery is a cultural reverie. Wander through its halls, where contemporary Moroccan art takes center stage. Special exhibitions often bring an extra layer of creativity to the space, turning your visit into an exploration of diverse expressions.

And then, as night falls, Pacha Marrakech comes alive. The iconic venue promises a nightlife extravaganza – imagine dancing under the stars to the beats of world-renowned DJs, surrounded by stylish interiors and an infectious energy that defines Hivernage after dark.

Kasbah

Step into the historical heart of Marrakesh with a visit to the Kasbah. This district is a living testament to the city's past, with its narrow streets, traditional riads, and historic landmarks. Explore the impressive Badi Palace, where remnants of grandeur offer a glimpse into Morocco's architectural heritage. The Saadian Tombs, hidden behind ancient walls, house ornate mausoleums and echoes of the city's regal history. The Kasbah invites you to wander through time, where each corner reveals the layers of Marrakesh's cultural tapestry.

What to do and see

Start your day in the Kasbah with Bahia Palace. This place is a sensory feast - vibrant gardens, intricate tiles, and a maze of rooms that feel like something out of a royal dream. Let yourself get lost in the beauty. Then, saunter over to El Badi Palace, a crumbling masterpiece that whispers tales of opulence from another era. You can almost imagine the grandeur of celebrations echoing through the now-ruined halls.

Next, let the Kasbah unfold its spiritual side at the Mouassine Mosque. You might not enter, but the minaret alone is a work of art against the blue sky. From there, weave through the Mellah, the Jewish Quarter. Its narrow streets are alive with the rhythm of daily life, and each door tells a story with its blue hue.

As you explore, dive into the spice-scented souks. These markets are a maze of colors and aromas. Textiles, ceramics, and spices – let your senses guide you. Engage with the sellers; they're often the best guides to hidden gems.

Now, it's time for a break. Find a café tucked in the alleys, order some mint tea, and just soak in the Kasbah vibes. These courtyards are like secret havens where time slows down, and you can catch your breath amidst the historical whirlwind.

Speaking of whirlwinds, let's get lost in the alleys again. Forget the map, let instinct be your guide. You might stumble upon hidden gems – perhaps a family-run bakery with the most delightful pastries or a tucked-away artisan workshop crafting wonders.

And don't forget to glance up; the Kasbah isn't just at eye level. Look at the intricacies of the doorways,

the play of light and shadow in the courtyards –
that's where the true charm lies.

Palmeraie

Escape the urban hustle and find serenity in
Palmeraie, the palm oasis just outside Marrakesh.
Picture a vast expanse of palm groves, luxury
resorts, and sprawling villas. Palmeraie offers a
tranquil retreat, with winding pathways leading you
through lush greenery. This district is a haven for
relaxation, where you can enjoy a round of golf,
unwind in a spa, or simply bask in the calm
surroundings. Palmeraie is a sanctuary that
complements the vibrant energy of Marrakesh.

What to do and see

Palmeraie Golf Palace welcomes you with open
arms. A luxurious resort adorned with traditional
Moroccan architecture, it's not just a place to stay;
it's an experience. Picture yourself teeing off on the
27-hole golf course, surrounded by the rustling of
palm leaves and the scent of blooming flowers. Take
a leisurely stroll around the manicured gardens, and
you might encounter the regal strut of peacocks,
adding a touch of whimsy to your stay.

For those seeking a taste of adventure, camel riding
excursions await. Traverse through palm groves,
feeling the gentle sway of the camel's gait. It's a
journey that transcends time, connecting you with
the age-old traditions of the desert. Capture the

picturesque moments, and consider each step a unique addition to your Marrakeshi memories.

Hidden within the oasis is the Palmeraie Museum, a treasure trove of Berber artifacts and art. Step into this cultural sanctuary, where each exhibit tells a story of Morocco's rich heritage. Engage with knowledgeable guides, and let the history of the Berber people unfold before you, adding depth to your understanding of this vibrant culture.

Palais Rhoul is not just a boutique hotel; it's a masterpiece of architecture and tranquility. Wander through its gardens adorned with fountains, and let the opulence of the surroundings transport you to a world of serenity. Consider a spa session as a rejuvenating interlude, allowing the soothing ambiance of Palmeraie to seep into your senses.

For the thrill-seekers, quad biking adventures beckon. Zoom through the palm groves, feel the rush of the wind, and let the adrenaline heighten your senses. Capture the exhilaration of your journey, and let it be a highlight reel of your Palmeraie escapade.

L'Oliveraie de Marigha, nestled within an olive grove, offers a culinary experience like no other. Savor traditional Moroccan cuisine amidst the greenery, creating a sensory fusion of flavors and ambiance. Reserve a table on the terrace for a panoramic view, and let each bite be a celebration of Moroccan culinary artistry.

Mellah

Discover Marrakesh's cultural diversity in Mellah, the historic Jewish quarter. As you traverse its narrow streets, observe the fusion of Moroccan and Jewish influences in the architecture and atmosphere. Mellah is a neighborhood that encapsulates centuries of coexistence, with synagogues like Lazama and lively markets showcasing a unique blend of traditions. Explore the cultural richness as you engage with locals and uncover the stories etched into the walls of this fascinating quarter.

What to do and see

Start your exploration at the magnificent Bahia Palace, a 19th-century marvel surrounded by lush gardens. Imagine wandering through its intricately decorated halls, where echoes of grandeur and opulence resonate. As you stroll through Mellah Souk, let the vibrant colors of textiles and the aroma of spices guide your way. Engage with local artisans, soak in the lively atmosphere, and discover the treasures hidden within the bustling market.

Next, venture into the Lazama Synagogue, a sacred sanctuary dating back to the 16th century. Feel the tranquility within its walls, and perhaps, if the timing is right, witness a moment of prayer or reflection. El Badi Palace, just a short walk away, offers a different spectacle – the remnants of a once-grand palace, with courtyards and gardens that invite contemplation.

Follow your senses to Mellah's culinary delights, where traditional Jewish pastries like "mofletta" await at local bakeries. Savor the flavors of sweet pastries and inhale the intoxicating scents of exotic spices as you meander through the historic quarter.

Wander through Mellah's residential streets, where historical residences stand as silent witnesses to centuries of stories. Imagine the lives that unfolded within these walls, the celebrations held, and the daily rhythms of generations past. Take a moment to appreciate the architectural blend of Moroccan, Jewish, and Andalusian influences that characterizes this neighborhood.

In Mellah, diversity isn't just a concept – it's a lived reality. Engage with locals, listen to their stories, and discover the harmonious coexistence of different communities. If your visit aligns with Jewish festivals, such as Hanukkah or Purim, immerse yourself in the lively celebrations that bring Mellah to life.

GETTING AROUND IN MARRAKESH

Marrakesh is a vibrant tapestry of sights and sounds. Ready for an adventure in this bustling Moroccan city? Let's get you there and navigating like a pro!

Getting to Marrakesh:

By Plane:

Marrakesh Menara Airport (RAK): This is your magical carpet ride into Marrakesh. It's around 6 kilometers (3.7 miles) southwest of the city center. As you land, be prepared for the warm embrace of Marrakesh's colors and energy.

From the Airport:

Taxi: The airport is well-connected to the city by taxis. Remember to negotiate the fare before starting your journey or ensure that the meter is running. The ride to the city center takes around 15-20 minutes.

Airport Shuttle: Some hotels offer shuttle services, making it a hassle-free option, especially if you've arranged accommodations beforehand.

Moving Around Marrakesh:

Jemaa el-Fnaa Square:

As the sun sets, this iconic square transforms into a vibrant spectacle. The air fills with the aroma of grilled meats and spices, while snake charmers, magicians, and storytellers entertain the crowds. It's a sensory overload!

Bus Stop: Jemaa el-Fnaa serves as a central hub for many local buses. Keep an eye out for signs or ask the locals for guidance on the nearest bus stops.

Koutoubia Mosque:

Standing tall against the skyline, the Koutoubia Mosque's minaret is a defining feature of Marrakesh. You can admire its architectural beauty from afar or take a moment for quiet reflection within its grounds.

Hop-On, Hop-Off Bus Stops: These tourist-friendly buses often have designated stops near major attractions like the Koutoubia Mosque, making it convenient for sightseeing.

Majorelle Garden:

Once owned by Yves Saint Laurent, these gardens are a serene escape from the city's hustle. The vibrant cobalt blue structures against the lush greenery make for an Instagram-worthy paradise.

Local Buses or Taxis: While not directly in the heart of the city, a taxi or local bus will get you to these gardens comfortably.

Souks in the Medina:

The maze-like streets of the Medina are home to the bustling souks. Lose yourself (figuratively!) in the colorful array of spices, leather goods, textiles, and handicrafts. Don't forget to haggle for the best deals!

Walking or Bicycle: Navigating the narrow alleys of the souks is best done on foot or by bicycle if you're feeling adventurous.

Bahia Palace:

Prepare to be awestruck by the intricate details and architectural wonders of Bahia Palace. With its stunning courtyards and ornate decorations, you'll feel transported to another era.

Taxi or Horse Carriage: Opt for a taxi or indulge in a traditional horse-drawn carriage ('caleche') for a royal entrance to this palace.

WHERE TO EAT IN MARRAKESH

Buckle up for a culinary adventure through Marrakesh's top restaurants! Get ready to tantalize your taste buds with flavors that'll make your stomach sing.

NOMAD

Menu Highlights: Start with their vibrant Moroccan salads like the beetroot, carrot, and orange salad—a burst of colors and flavors. Dive into their sumptuous lamb tagine, slow-cooked to perfection, or try their saffron chicken, a dish that's both fragrant and savory. And oh, their cocktails! The pomegranate mojito is a local favorite, perfectly balancing sweet and tangy notes.

Le Jardin

Menu Highlights: Picture yourself dining amidst a lush garden while relishing Moroccan delicacies. Indulge in their vegetable tagine, brimming with the flavors of slow-cooked vegetables and aromatic spices. Don't miss their lamb couscous, tender and seasoned to perfection. Wrap up your meal with mint tea, accompanied by heavenly pastries like baklava or almond-filled treats.

Café Arabe

Menu Highlights: A fusion of Moroccan and Italian cuisine awaits you here. Savor their aromatic couscous dishes, with options ranging from lamb to vegetable varieties. Explore their wood-fired pizzas topped with local ingredients for a unique twist. The cocktail menu is a treasure trove; try their Marrakesh Mule for a refreshing kick.

La Maison Arabe

Menu Highlights: Indulge in the authentic flavors of Morocco. Start with their traditional pastillas—layers of flaky pastry filled with savory delights. Their seven-vegetable couscous is a true masterpiece, each ingredient bursting with flavor. For dessert, delve into their decadent sweets like almond briouats or date-filled pastries.

Gastro MK at Maison MK

Menu Highlights: Get ready for an innovative tasting experience. Dive into their spiced lamb shoulder, slow-cooked to tender perfection and bursting with flavor. Their seafood dishes are a symphony of taste, often featuring fresh catches prepared with local spices. Save room for desserts that are as visually stunning as they are delicious.

Al Fassia

Menu Highlights: This gem celebrates Berber cuisine with a focus on tradition. Their couscous dishes are a must-try, featuring delicate grains paired with flavorful meats and vegetables. The slow-cooked tagines are rich and aromatic, transporting you to the heart of Moroccan cuisine. And the pastries? Pure indulgence.

Dar Moha

Menu Highlights: Discover a refined Moroccan feast here. Start with a pigeon pastilla, a delicate pastry filled with succulent pigeon meat and aromatic spices. Their lamb tagines are tender and flavorful, while the assorted mezze present a variety of tastes to delight your palate. Finish with desserts that are as artistic as they are delicious.

Amal Women's Training Center & Restaurant

Menu Highlights: Beyond the delicious food, this place supports a noble cause. Try their flavorful tagines, each brimming with authentic Moroccan spices and herbs. Their couscous specialties are a delight, and the desserts—a mix of traditional and innovative treats—are a sweet ending to a meaningful meal.

Grand Café de la Poste

Menu Highlights: Mixing French flair with Moroccan charm, this spot offers an array of seafood dishes, from perfectly grilled fish to seafood pastas. Their steaks are cooked to perfection and paired with savory sauces. Don't skip their

Moroccan pastries; they're a delightful way to conclude your meal.

Dar Yacout

Menu Highlights: Step into this mesmerizing riad for a truly immersive dining experience. Savor the aromatic lamb tagines, rich with spices and tender meat. The grilled fish is a flavorful delight. And the desserts? They're like a sweet symphony that wraps up your meal perfectly.

Direction

NOMAD

Address: Rahba Kedima, Marrakesh Medina

- Directions: From Jemaa el-Fnaa, head towards Rahba Kedima. NOMAD is located in the heart of the Medina. It's a short walk, and the vibrant atmosphere will guide you.

Le Jardin

Address: 32 Souk El Jeld Sidi Abdelaziz, Medina, Marrakesh

- Directions: Nestled within the Medina, Le Jardin is located near the Mouassine Fountain. Walk through the narrow streets, and the oasis-like setting will unfold before you.

Café Arabe

Address: 184 Rue Mouassine, Marrakesh Medina

- Directions: Wander through the streets near Mouassine Mosque, and you'll find Café Arabe. It's a charming walk through the Medina's lively alleys.

La Maison Arabe

Address: 1 Derb Assehbe, Marrakesh Medina

- Directions: Tucked away in the Medina, near Bab Doukkala, La Maison Arabe is a short walk from the city center. Follow signs to Bab Doukkala and navigate through the streets to find this gem.

Gastro MK at Maison MK

Address: 14 Derb Sebaai, Riad Laarous, Marrakesh Medina

- Directions: Situated in Riad Laarous, this restaurant is a bit further within the Medina. Navigate towards Riad Laarous, and the restaurant is within walking distance.

Al Fassia

Address: Boulevard Zerktouni, Quartier de l'Hivernage, Marrakesh

- Directions: Located in the Hivernage district, Al Fassia is a bit outside the Medina. It's best reached by taxi or a short ride from the city center.

Dar Moha

Address: 81 Rue Dar El Bacha, Marrakesh Medina

- Directions: Situated near the Dar El Bacha Palace, this restaurant is reachable by walking from the city center or a short taxi ride.

Amal Women's Training Center & Restaurant

Address: Rue Allal Ben Ahmed, Marrakesh Medina

- Directions: Located close to Bab Doukkala, navigate through the Medina's streets to find this heartwarming place supporting a noble cause.

Grand Café de la Poste

Address: Avenue Imam Malik, Gueliz, Marrakesh

- Directions: Situated in the Gueliz district, this restaurant is a short taxi ride or walk from the city center. Follow Avenue Imam Malik to reach the spot.

Dar Yacout

Address: 79 Sidi Ahmed Soussi, Marrakesh Medina

- Directions: Nestled within the Medina, Dar Yacout is a bit tucked away. Follow the signs or consider hiring a guide to navigate the labyrinthine streets to reach this mesmerizing riad.

TOP ATTRACTIONS IN MARRAKESH

The vibrant rhythm of Jemaa el-Fnaa Square beckons, and gardens bloom in vivid hues amidst palatial grandeur. Marrakesh, a city of kaleidoscopic allure, weaves tales of opulence, tradition, and cultural richness. Imagine strolling through bustling markets where snake charmers mesmerize, standing in awe of the majestic Koutoubia Mosque's towering minaret, and discovering tranquil oases like Majorelle Garden amidst the bustling streets. From the ornate Bahia Palace to the hidden treasures of the Mellah and the historic Saadian Tombs, each attraction is a chapter in Marrakesh's vibrant narrative, inviting you to immerse yourself in its colorful tapestry of sights and stories.

Jemaa el-Fnaa Square

The Heartbeat of Marrakesh: This iconic square is a mesmerizing whirlwind of activity. Picture snake charmers hypnotizing their serpentine companions, storytellers weaving ancient tales, and aromatic food stalls enticing you with their sizzling delicacies. As the sun sets, the square transforms into a lively spectacle, where the vibrant energy of Marrakesh truly comes alive.

Koutoubia Mosque

An Iconic Landmark: Dominating the skyline with its stunning minaret, the Koutoubia Mosque is not just a place of worship but an architectural marvel. The intricate geometric patterns and the imposing structure stand as a testament to the city's rich heritage and Islamic artistry.

Majorelle Garden

A Botanical Oasis: Step into this tranquil haven, where cobalt blue structures contrast with lush greenery. The Majorelle Garden is a painter's palette brought to life, with exotic plants, gurgling streams, and vibrant colors at every turn. It's a sanctuary that once captured the heart of Yves Saint Laurent.

Bahia Palace

A Majestic Residence: Walk through the intricate corridors and ornate rooms of the Bahia Palace. This architectural gem is a testament to Moroccan craftsmanship, with its intricate tile work, ornamental ceilings, and enchanting courtyards that whisper tales of grandeur and opulence.

Saadian Tombs

Historical Marvels: Discover the hidden treasure of the Saadian Tombs, where time stands still amidst the beautifully adorned chambers. These royal tombs are a remarkable blend of intricate tile work and serene tranquility, housing the remains of Saadian rulers and their families.

El Badi Palace

A Ruined Splendor: Explore the ruins of El Badi Palace, once a lavish complex adorned with precious materials and extravagant designs. While time has worn away its opulence, the sheer scale of the palace and the remnants of its grandeur offer a glimpse into Marrakesh's regal past.

The Mellah

A Historic Jewish Quarter: Wander through the Mellah, the historic Jewish quarter of Marrakesh. Discover its narrow alleys, hidden synagogues, and the echoes of a once-thriving community, offering a unique perspective on the city's diverse cultural tapestry.

Museum of Marrakesh

Art and Culture Unveiled: Step into the Museum of Marrakesh, housed in a stunning 19th-century palace. Admire the exhibits showcasing Moroccan art, traditional crafts, and artifacts that tell stories of the city's past, offering a glimpse into its rich cultural heritage.

Tanneries of Marrakesh

The Craftsmanship of Leather: Experience the ancient craft of leatherwork at the tanneries, where hides are transformed into vibrant leather goods. Witness artisans working amidst colorful vats of dyes, an age-old tradition that still thrives today.

Menara Gardens

Tranquil Reflections: Escape the bustling city and find solace in the Menara Gardens. The tranquil olive groves, reflective pools, and the backdrop of the Atlas Mountains create a serene setting, perfect for a leisurely stroll or a moment of quiet contemplation.

Dar Si Said Museum

Artistry Unveiled: Delve into Moroccan woodworking and craftsmanship at the Dar Si Said Museum. Admire intricately carved doors, traditional furniture, and artifacts that showcase the country's artisanal heritage.

Agdal Gardens

Symmetry in Nature: Lose yourself in the geometric perfection of the Agdal Gardens, where symmetrical orchards and reflective pools create a serene escape. This ancient royal garden is a testament to precision and beauty in landscaping.

TOP CUISINE TO TRY OUT IN MARRAKESH

From the ritual of pouring Moroccan mint tea to savoring crispy Sfenj doughnuts, each dish is a symphony of tastes inviting you to indulge in Marrakesh's vibrant gastronomic tapestry. Whether you're exploring the vibrant street food scene or sipping on the iconic Harira soup, these top cuisines are an invitation to savor the essence of Morocco's rich culinary heritage with every delectable bite.

Tagine Magic

Flavorful Delights: Ah, the iconic tagine! Picture a cone-shaped clay pot filled with tender meat, poultry, or vegetables, slow-cooked to perfection with aromatic spices like saffron, cumin, and cinnamon. Don't miss out on the lamb, chicken, or vegetable tagines that promise a symphony of flavors in every bite.

Couscous Extravaganza

Grainy Goodness: Indulge in the Moroccan staple, couscous! Delicately steamed and served with an array of toppings—tender meat, vegetables, and a burst of spices. The fluffy texture of the couscous paired with savory stews is a match made in culinary heaven.

Pastilla Pleasure

Savory & Sweet Fusion: Prepare your taste buds for pastilla, a delightful blend of sweet and savory. Layers of thin pastry stuffed with a delectable mix of spiced meat, almonds, and sometimes a hint of sweetness from powdered sugar and cinnamon. It's a mouthwatering experience you won't forget!

Moroccan Mint Tea

Tea Ceremony: Sip on the famed Moroccan mint tea, a ritual in itself. Watch as the tea is poured from a height, creating a frothy top. The sweetened green tea infused with fresh mint leaves is not just a drink—it's a gesture of hospitality and a refreshing respite from the bustling streets.

Mechoui Madness

Slow-Roasted Sensation: If you're a fan of succulent meats, Mechoui is a must-try! Picture a whole lamb or goat slow-roasted to juicy perfection, seasoned with a blend of spices, and served with bread. It's a carnivore's dream come true.

Street Food Frenzy

Vibrant Bites: Embrace the lively street food scene! From sizzling skewers of kebabs and merguez sausages to crispy fried fish sandwiches and flavorful snail soup, the streets of Marrakesh are a treasure trove of delectable bites waiting to be savored.

Harira Heaven

Satisfying Soup: Dive into the heartiness of Harira, a traditional soup often enjoyed during Ramadan. This comforting blend of tomatoes, lentils, chickpeas, and aromatic spices warms the soul with its rich flavors.

Satisfy with Sfenj

Doughy Delights: Treat yourself to Sfenj, Moroccan doughnuts that are crispy on the outside and soft on the inside. These deep-fried dough rings coated in sugar are an absolute delight for anyone with a sweet tooth.

Fresh Fruits & Juices

Colorful Refreshment: Don't miss out on the abundance of fresh fruits and juices. Sample the vibrant array of oranges, pomegranates, dates, and other seasonal fruits, either as a snack or freshly squeezed into a refreshing drink.

Sweet Treats Galore

Indulgent Desserts: End your culinary journey on a sweet note with Moroccan desserts like Baklava, delicate pastries filled with nuts and sweetened with honey or sugar syrup. Or try the melt-in-your-mouth delight of Halwa Shebakia, fried dough dipped in honey.

FESTIVAL AND EVENTS IN MARRAKESH

Get ready to dive into Marrakesh's festive vibes, where the city comes alive with a whirlwind of colors, music, and cultural flair. Imagine a calendar brimming with celebrations that infuse the air with an infectious energy, inviting locals and visitors alike to join in the revelry:

Marrakesh Popular Arts Festival

Showtime Extravaganza: Marrakesh kicks off the party with its Popular Arts Festival! Think of it as a grand spectacle where the city transforms into a stage for musicians, dancers, and artists from across Morocco and the world. Streets buzz with vibrant performances, turning every corner into a surprise celebration of local culture.

Rose Festival in El Kelaa M'Gouna

Petal-Painted Paradise: Just a stone's throw from Marrakesh lies El Kelaa M'Gouna, where the Rose Festival blooms. Immerse yourself in a flowery wonderland as the valley erupts in jubilation, celebrating the harvest of fragrant roses with parades, dances, and a lively Rose Queen ceremony.

Eid Celebrations

Feast & Festivity: The city gets into high gear during Eid al-Fitr and Eid al-Adha! Imagine bustling markets filled with delectable treats, families gathering for sumptuous feasts, and mosques resonating with prayers and joyful celebrations, marking the end of Ramadan and the Hajj pilgrimage.

National Day of Morocco

Red & Green Revelry: Morocco's National Day paints Marrakesh in patriotic colors! Streets adorned with flags, vibrant parades, cultural performances, and perhaps a sprinkle of fireworks in the night sky—all in celebration of the country's unity and heritage.

Fantasia Festival

Equestrian Spectacle: Saddle up for the Fantasia Festival, a dazzling display of horsemanship and tradition. Watch in awe as riders, adorned in traditional attire, perform thrilling equestrian feats involving synchronized riding and spectacular rifle shooting.

Imilchil Marriage Festival

Love & Unity: Head to the Atlas Mountains for a unique celebration of love at the Imilchil Marriage Festival. Witness the ancient Berber tradition where couples find love and unity, marking the occasion with colorful ceremonies, music, and dances that echo the spirit of the region.

International Film Festival of Marrakech

Hollywood Glamour: It's Marrakesh's time to shine on the silver screen! A star-studded affair unfolds with red carpets, film screenings, and discussions on cinema, attracting cinephiles and celebrities from around the globe.

Marrakesh Marathon

Run & Cheer: Lace up those running shoes for the Marrakesh Marathon! Join the marathon madness, where the city's streets become a playground for runners and spectators alike, blending athletic prowess with community spirit.

Gnaoua World Music Festival in Essaouira

Melodic Fusion: Though a short trip away, the Gnaoua World Music Festival in Essaouira deserves a spot on your festival calendar. Revel in the mesmerizing beats and spiritual music of the Gnaoua people, blending traditional African melodies with contemporary tunes.

Djemaa el-Fnaa Daily Celebrations

Street Magic Every Day: While not an official festival, Djemaa el-Fnaa Square is an ongoing carnival! Imagine a daily extravaganza with snake charmers, storytellers, bustling food stalls, and lively performances—a vibrant celebration of Marrakesh's cultural richness.

TOP ACCOMMODATION IN MARRAKESH

Imagine your stay in Marrakesh as an adventure in itself, where your accommodation becomes a part of the city's vibrant charm.

La Mamounia

Palatial Paradise: Enter a world of luxury at La Mamounia, where opulence meets Moroccan elegance. With stunning gardens, lavish interiors, and a spa fit for royalty, this iconic hotel is a haven of indulgence.

Royal Mansour Marrakech

Regal Retreat: Indulge in absolute luxury in your own private riad at the Royal Mansour Marrakech. With personalized service, exquisite decor, and opulent amenities, it's a sanctuary that whispers tales of grandeur.

Riad Joya

Boutique Chic: Step into Riad Joya, a hidden gem in the heart of the Medina. This boutique riad oozes charm with its intimate ambiance, intricate designs, and personalized service that makes you feel like royalty.

Amanjena

Tranquil Oasis: Amanjena invites you to an oasis of calm with its serene surroundings and minimalist elegance. With its stunning pavilions, serene pools, and impeccable service, it's a retreat for the soul.

El Fenn

Artistic Haven: Experience the eclectic charm of El Fenn, a boutique hotel adorned with contemporary art and vibrant interiors. Its rooftop terrace offers panoramic views, and each corner is a celebration of creativity.

Sofitel Marrakech Lounge and Spa

Modern Comfort: Immerse yourself in modern luxury at Sofitel Marrakech. Enjoy the blend of Moroccan architecture and contemporary design, along with its lush gardens and tranquil pools.

Les Jardins de la Koutoubia

Majestic Elegance: Discover Les Jardins de la Koutoubia, nestled near the iconic Koutoubia Mosque. This hotel exudes traditional Moroccan charm with its ornate decor and lush gardens.

Palais Namaskar

Zen Paradise: Palais Namaskar offers a luxurious escape surrounded by tranquility. With its serene ponds, elegant villas, and world-class amenities, it's a sanctuary for relaxation.

Riad Kniza

Historic Charm: Riad Kniza blends history with hospitality. Experience the warmth of Moroccan hospitality in this restored riad, where intricate designs and antique furnishings create an ambiance of timeless elegance.

Mandarin Oriental, Marrakech

Modern Serenity: Enter a world of contemporary luxury at Mandarin Oriental. Surrounded by lush gardens and serene pools, this haven offers a perfect blend of modern comforts and Moroccan allure.

Selman Marrakech

Equestrian Elegance: Selman Marrakech boasts an equestrian theme with stunning Arabian horse stables. From its lavish decor to the tranquil setting, it's a retreat that exudes luxury and sophistication.

Riad Dar Anika

Intimate Charm: Dive into the intimate charm of Riad Dar Anika, where personalized service and elegant design create a cozy oasis in the heart of Marrakesh's Medina.

SHOPPINMG IN MARRAKESH

Embark on a shopping adventure in Marrakesh's bustling souks and stylish boutiques. From the vibrant textiles of the medina to the intricate craftsmanship of leather goods, each market stall is a treasure trove waiting to be discovered. Get ready to haggle, explore, and bring home unique treasures that capture the essence of Marrakesh's vibrant marketplace.

Haggling 101:

Haggling is an art form in Marrakesh, and the souks are your canvas. Engage in the time-honored tradition of negotiating prices with the friendly local vendors. Remember, it's not just about the purchase; it's about the lively banter and forging a connection with the people. Be prepared to charm your way to a good deal, and don't forget to smile!

The Majestic Jardin Majorelle:

Escape the hustle and bustle of the souks for a moment of tranquility at the Jardin Majorelle. This stunning garden, once owned by Yves Saint Laurent, is a sanctuary of exotic plants, vibrant cobalt blue structures, and a boutique offering high-end Moroccan fashion and accessories. It's a serene shopping experience surrounded by beauty.

Moroccan Carpets:

No trip to Marrakesh is complete without bringing home a piece of its rich textile heritage. Explore the carpet shops where a kaleidoscope of Berber patterns and colors awaits. Each rug tells a story, and finding the perfect one is like discovering a hidden gem. Embrace the opportunity to learn about the ancient art of carpet making and choose a masterpiece to adorn your home.

Spices and Sensations in the Spice Souk:

Let your nose guide you through the aromatic Spice Souk, where mounds of vibrant spices create a feast for the senses. Inhale the fragrant scents of cumin, coriander, and saffron as you browse the colorful stalls. Pick up a selection of spices to recreate the flavors of Morocco in your own kitchen and make your culinary journey last long after you've left.

Artisanal Marvels in the Medina:

Wander deeper into the heart of the Medina to discover hidden artisan workshops where skilled craftsmen create exquisite pieces. From handcrafted leather goods and traditional pottery to intricate metalwork, each shop is a testament to the city's rich artistic heritage. Marvel at the craftsmanship and take home a piece of Marrakesh's soul.

Fashion Finds in Gueliz:

Step into the modern side of Marrakesh by exploring the trendy district of Gueliz. Here, chic boutiques and contemporary art galleries coexist with traditional markets. Unleash your inner fashionista as you browse through stylish Moroccan designer stores, featuring a fusion of traditional craftsmanship and modern aesthetics. Gueliz offers a perfect blend of the city's historic charm and cosmopolitan flair.

Explore the Night Markets:

As the sun sets and the city transforms into a magical realm, the night markets come alive with a different energy. Head to Jemaa el-Fnaa square, where an eclectic array of stalls emerges, offering everything from handmade jewelry to intricate lanterns. The atmosphere is electric, with storytellers, musicians, and street performers creating a lively ambiance that adds a touch of enchantment to your shopping experience.

Sip Mint Tea at a Local Café:

Amidst your shopping escapades, take a moment to unwind and soak in the local atmosphere at a traditional Moroccan café. Order a cup of mint tea, a staple of Moroccan hospitality, and enjoy the bustling scene around you. Engaging with locals over a cup of tea can lead to unexpected discoveries, whether it's a hidden gem of a shop or a fascinating story about the city.

Souvenir Shopping at Ensemble Artisanal:

For a curated shopping experience, head to Ensemble Artisanal, a government-sponsored cooperative where you can find a wide array of quality handmade goods. From leather goods and textiles to ceramics and jewelry, this is a one-stop destination for authentic Moroccan craftsmanship. It's an excellent choice for those seeking high-quality souvenirs with a guarantee of authenticity.

Discover Hidden Riad Boutiques:

Marrakesh's riads, traditional Moroccan houses with interior gardens, often hide secret boutiques within their ornate walls. Wander through the charming alleys, and you may stumble upon intimate shops showcasing unique clothing, accessories, and home decor. These hidden gems offer an exclusive shopping experience, where each item tells a story of artistry and culture.

Unwind at a Hammam and Spa:

After a day of exploring Marrakesh's shopping wonders, treat yourself to a rejuvenating experience at a traditional hammam and spa. Indulge in a spa day featuring Moroccan beauty products, argan oil treatments, and handmade soaps. It's not just about shopping for goods but also about investing in a holistic experience that leaves you refreshed and revitalized.

MARRAKESH VIBRANT NIGHTLIFE

As the sun sets, Marrakesh transforms into a nightlife haven where the city's energy takes center stage. From the chic lounges of Gueliz to the lively beats of rooftop bars overlooking the medina, the city's nightlife is a symphony of lights and sounds.

Pacha Marrakech - The Iconic Party Palace:

Kick off your night at Pacha Marrakech, a legendary venue with a global reputation. Nestled in the heart of the city, this high-energy club boasts a glamorous atmosphere, top-notch DJs, and a crowd ready to groove. Let the world-renowned Pacha experience set the tone for an unforgettable night.

Theatro Marrakech - Where Fantasy Meets Nightlife:

Step into Theatro Marrakech, a club that transcends traditional nightlife. This theatrical venue combines stunning visuals, immersive performances, and a diverse music selection. Expect the unexpected as you dance under mesmerizing lights and lose yourself in the fantasy of the night.

555 Famous Club - Moroccan Elegance Meets International Beats:

Experience the perfect blend of Moroccan charm and international flair at 555 Famous Club. With its luxurious setting and a mix of global and local DJs, this venue promises an extraordinary night out. Immerse yourself in the vibrant ambiance and dance to beats that echo the spirit of Marrakesh.

Comptoir Darna - A Nightclub with Moroccan Soul:

Comptoir Darna is not just a club; it's a cultural experience. This Marrakesh institution seamlessly blends traditional Moroccan elements with a modern nightclub setting. Enjoy live music, belly dancing performances, and a menu featuring local delicacies. It's a place where the past and present collide on the dancefloor.

The Moroccan House Hotel - Extravagance Redefined:

For an opulent and exclusive experience, head to The Moroccan House Hotel. This venue is not just a club; it's a lifestyle. Indulge in luxury as you dance to the beats of international DJs in a setting that oozes sophistication and glamour.

Bo & Zin - Fusion of Music and Exotic Vibes:

Escape the ordinary at Bo & Zin, a club that seamlessly blends world music with exotic vibes. This unique venue offers a relaxed yet lively atmosphere, making it the perfect spot to unwind with friends or dance to a diverse range of beats.

Jad Mahal - Moroccan Grandeur with a Modern Twist:

Jad Mahal is a sensory feast that combines Moroccan grandeur with contemporary beats. Set in a lavish palace, this club offers an eclectic mix of music, live performances, and an ambiance that transports you to a world where every moment is a celebration.

The Cabaret - Where Glam Meets Entertainment:

Step into The Cabaret for a night of glamour and entertainment. This club goes beyond the ordinary with its cabaret-style shows, dazzling performances, and a dancefloor that beckons you to unleash your inner star. Get ready for a night of extravagance and non-stop fun.

Skybar - Rooftop Revelry with a View:

Elevate your night at Skybar, a rooftop venue offering panoramic views of Marrakesh. Sip on exotic cocktails while dancing under the stars, surrounded by a chic and cosmopolitan crowd. It's the perfect blend of sophistication and excitement, all with a breathtaking backdrop.

Kosybar - Bohemian Vibes and Live Music:

For a more laid-back but equally vibrant experience, head to Kosybar. This bohemian hotspot combines a relaxed atmosphere with live music, creating the perfect setting to unwind with friends. Enjoy the eclectic tunes and the company of fellow free spirits.

Lotus Club - A Nightclub Oasis:

Lotus Club is a hidden gem in the heart of Marrakesh, known for its lush garden setting and a dancefloor that comes alive after dark. With a mix of local and international DJs, this club offers a unique blend of Moroccan hospitality and global beats.

6th Sense Club - Where Intuition Meets Rhythm:

Let your sixth sense guide you to 6th Sense Club, a venue where intuition meets rhythm. This intimate club is a haven for music lovers, with an eclectic playlist that caters to diverse tastes. Immerse yourself in the sounds and let the music take control.

Le Salama - Rooftop Revelry in the Medina:

Le Salama is not just a club; it's a journey through the heart of the Medina. With a rooftop terrace offering stunning views, this venue is a delightful blend of traditional Moroccan charm and modern beats. Dance the night away surrounded by the beauty of Marrakesh.

The Source Marrakech - Oasis of Electronic Beats:

Electronic music enthusiasts, look no further than The Source Marrakech. This club, set in a lush garden, is a haven for those who crave cutting-edge beats and a vibrant atmosphere. Get ready for a night of electronic euphoria under the starlit sky.

Epicurien Club - Intimate Vibes, Big Energy:

Close your night with a visit to Epicurien Club, a venue that captures the essence of Marrakesh's nightlife in an intimate setting. With its energetic crowd, stylish decor, and a dancefloor that beckons, it's the perfect finale to your club-hopping adventure.

10 AMAZING ITENERARIES IN MARRAKESH

Embark on a journey through Marrakesh's diverse landscapes with 10 amazing itineraries catering to every traveler's preference. Whether you're a history buff exploring ancient palaces, a foodie delving into culinary delights, or an art enthusiast savoring local crafts, each itinerary is a curated adventure waiting to unfold. Get ready to explore Marrakesh your way.

The Timeless Explorer:
Day 1:

Morning: Begin your day with the call to prayer echoing from the Koutoubia Mosque. Marvel at its exquisite architecture and explore the nearby Cyber Park for a tranquil start.

Afternoon: Head to Jemaa el-Fnaa, the beating heart of Marrakesh. Lose yourself in the lively souks, where each alley reveals a new treasure. Don't miss the bustling Rahba Kedima square for an authentic spice market experience.

Evening: Wander through the enchanting Jardin Majorelle, designed by Yves Saint Laurent. The vibrant blue structures and exotic plants create a serene atmosphere. Wrap up your day with a traditional Moroccan dinner in a riad.

The Bohemian Art Aficionado:
Day 1:

Morning: Explore Gueliz's art scene on Rue de la Liberté, home to contemporary art galleries like David Bloch Gallery. Discover vibrant street art and trendy boutiques.

Afternoon: Visit the Le Jardin Secret, an artistic haven in the heart of the Medina. Stroll through its gardens and admire the restored architecture. Continue your artistic journey by exploring hidden gems in riad boutiques.

Evening: Conclude your day with a visit to Ensemble Artisanal, where curated, authentic crafts showcase Morocco's artistic richness.

The Night Market Maverick:

Evening Adventure:

Nightfall: As the sun sets, head to Jemaa el-Fnaa. Dive into the vibrant night market, where the air is filled with aromatic spices and the sounds of storytellers, musicians, and street performers.

Dinner: Try traditional street food, from savory tagines to delectable pastries. Engage with locals and haggle for unique souvenirs, turning the night market into your personal shopping spree.

The Luxe Shopper's Paradise:
Day 1:

Morning: Indulge in a luxurious shopping spree in Gueliz. Explore Avenue Mohammed V for high-end boutiques, featuring international and Moroccan designers.

Afternoon: Visit the YSL boutique in Jardin Majorelle for exclusive fashion and accessories. Explore the designer side of the Medina with hidden riad boutiques offering unique, upscale creations.

The Culinary Connoisseur:
Day 1:

Evening at Jemaa el-Fnaa: Begin your culinary adventure with a stroll through the food stalls of Jemaa el-Fnaa. Try local delicacies, from lamb tagines to freshly squeezed orange juice.

Day 2: Take a cooking class to master the art of Moroccan cuisine. Visit local markets to source fresh ingredients and learn the secrets of preparing flavorful dishes. Cap off your day with a refined dinner in a beautiful riad.

The Nature Escapist:
Day Trip:

Morning: Head to the Ourika Valley for a day of nature exploration. Hike through the Atlas

Mountains, passing traditional Berber villages and enjoying breathtaking views.

Afternoon: Relax by the Ourika waterfalls, surrounded by the serene beauty of nature. Enjoy a traditional Berber meal with warm hospitality.

Evening: Return to Marrakesh, reinvigorated from a day spent in the natural wonders surrounding the city.

The Spa and Serenity Seeker:
Day of Bliss:

Morning: Begin your day with a serene yoga session at Jardin Majorelle. Connect with your surroundings and find inner peace.

Afternoon: Indulge in a spa day, experiencing traditional hammam treatments and massages using Moroccan beauty products.

Evening: End your day with a quiet dinner at a riad, savoring the tranquility that Marrakesh can offer.

The Adventure Aficionado:
Day of Thrills:

Morning: Soar above the Atlas Mountains in a hot air balloon at sunrise, taking in breathtaking views.

Afternoon: Land and explore the mountains on an ATV or camel trek, experiencing the rugged beauty of the landscape.

Evening: Conclude your adventurous day with a traditional Moroccan feast in a desert camp under the stars.

The Night Owl's Delight:
Evening Exploration:

Nightfall: Explore the vibrant nightlife of Gueliz. Start with rooftop bars like Sky Lounge, offering panoramic views of the city.

Late Evening: Immerse yourself in live music at venues like Theatro and dance the night away in stylish nightclubs such as Pacha Marrakech.

The Architectural Admirer:
Day 1:

Morning: Explore the historical architecture of the Medina, including the Saadian Tombs with their intricate tilework and the Bahia Palace showcasing stunning gardens and architecture.

Afternoon: Venture into the modern side of Marrakesh with a visit to the Royal Mansour, an architectural masterpiece known for its opulent design.

Evening: Conclude your day at La Mamounia, another architectural gem where tradition meets luxury. Enjoy the breathtaking surroundings and savor a meal in its exquisite restaurants.

IDEAL VISITING TIME

Timing is everything in Marrakesh, and the ideal visiting time is your ticket to a perfect adventure. From the bloom-filled spring, where the city comes alive with colors, to the cozy winter, ideal for savoring warm tagines by the fire, discover when Marrakesh shines the brightest

Spring: The Blossoming Bouquet of Colors

When: March to May

Weather: Spring in Marrakesh is like nature's grand unveiling after the cool winter months. Days are comfortably warm, ranging between 15-25°C (59-77°F), making it ideal for outdoor explorations. Evenings retain a pleasant coolness.

Highlights:

- Jardin Majorelle: The iconic garden, once owned by Yves Saint Laurent, is a symphony of colors in spring. Bougainvillea, cacti, and other exotic flora burst into bloom, creating a mesmerizing palette.
- Festivals: Don't miss the Rose Festival in Kelaa Mgouna, where the air is infused with the delicate scent of roses. Streets are adorned with vibrant petals, celebrating the harvest.

Summer: Sun-Kissed Adventures

When: June to August

Weather: Summer in Marrakesh is characterized by abundant sunshine and temperatures ranging from 20-40°C (68-104°F). Days can be hot, but evenings bring a refreshing coolness, creating a delightful contrast.

Highlights:

- Rooftop Cafés: Embrace the warmth and soak in panoramic views from Marrakesh's numerous rooftop cafés. Sip on mint tea or freshly squeezed orange juice as you take in the cityscape.
- Atlas Mountains: Escape the summer heat with a day trip to the Atlas Mountains. Explore the picturesque valleys and Berber villages, where the temperature is more moderate.

Autumn: Harvesting Memories

When: September to November

Weather: Autumn brings a gentle transition from the summer heat to cooler temperatures, ranging from 15-30°C (59-86°F). The city is adorned with the warm hues of fall foliage, creating a picturesque setting.

Highlights:

- Local Markets: The souks come alive with preparations for festivals like Eid al-Adha.

Experience the vibrant atmosphere as locals shop for traditional clothing, spices, and gifts.

- Desert Excursions: Autumn is an ideal time for desert excursions. Venture into the Sahara for camel treks, stargazing, and a taste of nomadic life.

Winter: A Cozy Escape

When: December to February

Weather: Winter in Marrakesh is mild and comfortable, with daytime temperatures around 10-20°C (50-68°F). Evenings can be cool, creating a cozy atmosphere for exploration.

Highlights:

- Festive Atmosphere: Experience the magic of Marrakesh as it gets decked out for the holiday season. Streets are adorned with lights and decorations, creating a festive ambiance.
- Snow-Capped Atlas Mountains: Enjoy the breathtaking view of the Atlas Mountains draped in snow, adding a touch of winter wonderland charm to the city.

KEEPSAKES TO BRING BACK FROM MARRAKESH

Turn your Marrakesh journey into tangible memories with keepsakes that capture the city's essence. From vibrant ceramics to intricate metal lanterns, each item is a piece of Marrakesh waiting to adorn your home.

Moroccan Lanterns: Illuminate Your Memories

Why settle for ordinary lighting when you can have a Moroccan lantern casting whimsical patterns across your room? Picture the metalwork catching the sunlight, echoing the intricate beauty of the Koutoubia Mosque. Choose one that winks at you, as if saying, "I'll light up your world like the Marrakesh night sky."

Berber Carpets: Weaving Stories for Your Floor

The souks are a treasure trove of Berber carpets, each a storyteller in wool. Run your fingers over the patterns – symbols of Berber traditions and tales. It's not just a rug; it's a narrative waiting to unfold in your living room. Haggle with a playful spirit, as if unraveling the secrets woven into the threads.

Traditional Tagines: Cook Up Moroccan Magic at Home

Close your eyes and imagine the aroma of tagines wafting through the air. Now, bring that magic home with a traditional tagine. It's not just a clay pot; it's a vessel to recreate the flavors of Marrakesh in your kitchen. Choose one with a playful bargaining dance, as if haggling for spices in a bustling souk.

Leather Goods: Carry a Piece of Marrakesh in Style

Marrakesh is a leather lover's haven. From bags to belts, each piece is a work of art. Pick one that not only complements your style but also carries the whispers of the souks. Picture yourself negotiating with a twinkle in your eye, sealing the deal like a seasoned trader.

Argan Oil Products: Beauty Secrets from Morocco

Argan oil, the liquid gold of Morocco, holds the beauty secrets of Marrakesh. From skincare to haircare, bring back a piece of the Moroccan beauty regimen. It's not just a keepsake; it's a daily ritual that echoes the pampering of a traditional hammam. Picture yourself in serene steam, surrounded by the scents of argan oil.

Babouche Slippers: Dance through Life in Moroccan Style

Babouche slippers are more than footwear; they are a celebration of comfort and elegance. Choose a pair that adds a dash of Morocco to lazy days at home or your everyday adventures. Slip into the bargaining dance – find the perfect pair and let the shopkeeper join you in the rhythm.

Henna Art: Adorn Your Skin with Moroccan Elegance

Henna art isn't just a temporary tattoo; it's a celebration of intricate designs and Moroccan traditions. Bring back a henna kit and adorn your skin with patterns that tell your unique story. Channel your inner artist and design your own henna masterpiece.

Hand-Painted Ceramics: Sip Moroccan Magic

Moroccan ceramics are bursts of color and artistry. From tea sets to decorative plates, each piece is hand-painted with love. Choose something that will make your tea time a daily Moroccan ritual. Sip mint tea and reminisce about the bustling souks where you found your perfect ceramic set.

Traditional Kaftans: Wrap Yourself in Moroccan Chic

Kaftans are not just garments; they are a fashion statement. Flowy and adorned with vibrant colors and patterns, they capture the essence of Moroccan style. Bring one back to infuse your wardrobe with Marrakesh flair. Strut your stuff and haggle with a sense of runway drama as you choose the perfect kaftan.

Calligraphy Art: Words of Wisdom from Marrakesh

Moroccan calligraphy transforms words into visual poetry. Bring back a piece of calligraphy that resonates with you – whether it's a phrase, a quote, or a name – and let it inspire you daily. Negotiate with a poetic spirit, as if you're bargaining for a piece of someone's soul.

MARRAKESH VOCABULARY AND COMMON PHRASE

Unlock the door to authentic interactions with Marrakesh's locals by learning essential vocabulary and common phrases. From greetings that warm the heart to bargaining phrases that make you a souk expert, this language guide is your key to connecting with the city's soul.

Greetings – Welcoming the Marrakeshi Way:

- Hello - Salaam Aleikum: Start your interactions with the traditional Arabic greeting. Locals will appreciate your effort to embrace their culture.
- Response - Aleikum Salaam: The friendly reply to "Salaam Aleikum." It's the Moroccan way of saying, "Peace be upon you too."

Polite Pleasantries – Adding a Touch of Politeness:

- Thank You - Shukran: Express gratitude the Moroccan way. When someone offers assistance or hospitality, a sincere "Shukran" goes a long way.
- You're Welcome - Afwan: Respond graciously when someone thanks you. It's the Moroccan way of saying, "You're welcome."

Basic Numbers – Navigating the Souks:

- One - Wahid, Two - Juj, Three - Tlata: Mastering these numbers is your ticket to successful bargaining in the souks.
- How Much? - Bishhal?: Essential for shopping adventures. Use it with a curious smile as you explore the treasures in the market.

Foodie Phrases – Savoring Moroccan Delicacies:

- Delicious - Zween: When indulging in the delectable Moroccan cuisine, let out a satisfied "Zween" to compliment the chef.
- I'm Full - Shab L'ba: After a feast, use this phrase to politely decline more servings.

Directions – Navigating the Medina Maze:

- Where is...? - Fin huwa...?: Handy when exploring the labyrinthine alleys. Insert the name of your destination for a personalized map.
- Left - L'ecchel, Right - L'ymeen: Master these for seamless navigation through the maze-like Medina.

Bargaining Banter – Mastering the Souk Dance:

- Too Expensive - Ghali bzzaf: Use this phrase with a friendly smile to kick off the bargaining tango.
- Final Price? - Bhal taslouka?: When you're ready to seal the deal, ask for the final price with a twinkle in your eye.

Emergencies – Navigating the Unexpected:

- Help! - Musaada!: When in need, call for help with a clear and urgent "Musaada!"
- Where is the Hospital? - Fin huwa lmoustashfa?: Essential in case of emergencies.

Compliments – Spreading Moroccan Sunshine:

- Beautiful - Jamila: Shower compliments generously. From people to places, use "Jamila" to spread positivity.
- Nice - Mzyan: Appreciate everything from a tasty dish to a well-crafted souvenir with a simple "Mzyan."

Expressing Curiosity – Embracing the Local Vibes:

- What is This? - Shno hada?: Perfect for when you encounter something intriguing or unfamiliar. Use it with an inquisitive smile.

Farewells – Bid Adieu with Moroccan Charm:

- Goodbye - Bslama: As you leave a place or bid farewell to newfound friends, use this term for a Moroccan-flavored goodbye.
- See You Later - Wela nesmaa sbaah lkhir: If you plan on returning, express your intention to meet again with this phrase.

Street Smarts – Navigating Social Etiquette:

- Excuse Me - Smehli: Maneuver through crowded souks with polite "Smehli" requests.
- Sorry - Smahti: If you accidentally bump into someone or make a minor mishap, say "Smahti" with a apologetic nod.

Cultural Connections – Bridging the Cultural Gap:

- I Love Morocco - Kanbghik bladna: Express your love for the country with this heartfelt phrase.
- Moroccan Hospitality - Al hosn al maghribi: Acknowledge and appreciate the legendary hospitality with a nod and a smile.

Playful Exclamations – Adding Flair to Conversations:

- Wow! - Wahwah!: Express awe and admiration with this exclamation. Perfect for encounters with stunning architecture or delightful surprises.
- Fantastic! - Mrawej!: Use this enthusiastic term to celebrate anything from a great bargain to a delicious meal.

Weather Whimsy – Talking About the Elements:

- It's Hot - Skhoun: When the sun is shining brightly, let everyone know you're feeling the warmth.
- It's Cold - Bared: If you're experiencing a chilly evening, use "Bared" to describe the weather.

Making Friends – Opening Your Heart to Marrakeshi Souls:

- Can I Take a Photo? - Wach bgha nakhod soura?: Before capturing a moment, seek permission with this polite request.
- What's Your Name? - Shno smiytk?: Connect with locals on a personal level by asking their names.

Coffee Culture – Energizing Your Conversations:

- Coffee, Please - Qahwa, Afak: When you need a caffeine fix, use this phrase with a smile to order the beloved Moroccan coffee.
- Thank You for the Coffee - Shukran 'ala Qahwatk: Express gratitude for a delightful coffee experience.

Nightlife Lingo – Embracing Evening Adventures:

- Where's the Night Market? - Fin huwa suuq layl?: For those seeking the lively ambiance of Marrakesh after dark.
- This Place is Amazing! - Hadak lmakan wahed wahed!: Express your enthusiasm for a fantastic nightspot.

Nature Conversations – Appreciating the Landscape:

- Beautiful View - Manzar Jamil: Use this phrase to admire scenic landscapes or picturesque spots in and around Marrakesh.
- Is it Always Sunny? - Wach daiman chi shems?: Engage in casual weather chats and soak in the Moroccan sunshine.

Expressing Admiration – Showering Compliments Galore:

- Your Shop is Beautiful - Dukanek Jamil: When exploring the local shops, share your admiration for the charming storefronts.

- I Love Moroccan Crafts - Kanbghik El Fnane Maghribia: Celebrate the exquisite craftsmanship of Morocco with this affectionate phrase.

Relaxing Interactions – Unwinding Marrakeshi Style:

- Can I Sit Here? - Wach bgha nqaa hna?: Seek a cozy spot in a cafe or a communal space with this polite inquiry.
- What a Cozy Place! - Hadak lmakan kraii: Express your comfort and satisfaction with the welcoming atmosphere.

Festival Phrases – Immersing in Local Celebrations:

- Happy Festival! - Eid Mubarak!: Extend warm wishes during festive seasons and special occasions.
- What's Happening Today? - Wach kayn chi haja lyuma?: Stay informed about local events and festivities.

Transportation Talks – Navigating Marrakesh's Mobility:

- How Much is the Taxi? - Bishhal taxi?: Before hopping into a taxi, ensure a smooth ride by negotiating the fare.

- Could You Drop Me Here? - Wach ghadi nkhalik hna?: Use this phrase to communicate your preferred drop-off location.

Wildlife Encounters – Embracing Marrakesh's Fauna:

- Look at the Cats! - Chouf lqottat!: Marrakesh has a charming feline population; celebrate their presence with delight.
- Is It Safe to Approach Animals? - Wach kayn aman nhayad l'hyawan?: Ensure a respectful interaction with local animals.

Art Appreciation – Celebrating Marrakesh's Creativity:

- This Artwork is Stunning - Hadchi lfnane wahed wahed: When exploring galleries or artisan spaces, express your admiration for the creative pieces.
- What Inspired You? - Wach kaykhdmek?: Engage with local artists by expressing curiosity about their inspirations.

Souk Etiquette – Mastering the Shopping Scene:

- May I Browse? - Wach ghadi ntfarraj?: Politely ask for permission before exploring the treasures in a shop.

- I'm Just Looking - Ana ghir kandour: Communicate your browsing intentions with a casual yet friendly phrase.

Market Musings – Engaging in Vendor Banter:

- What's Special Today? - Wach kayn khossosi lyuma?: Get the inside scoop on unique finds and special deals from enthusiastic vendors.
- Tell Me About This - Goulili 3la hadchi: Encourage vendors to share stories about their products – it adds a personal touch to your shopping experience.

Magical Moments – Capturing the Essence of Marrakesh:

- This Feels Magical - Hadchi kaykoun wahed wahed: When you stumble upon a hidden gem or experience something extraordinary, let this phrase capture the enchantment.
- It's Like a Dream - Kanmout kifach rahto: Express your awe when reality feels as surreal as a dream.

Camaraderie Building – Connecting with Fellow Travelers:

- Where Are You From? - Menin jay? Break the ice with fellow travelers and exchange stories about your respective journeys.

- Let's Explore Together - Ghir nsafro m3a b3d: Extend an invitation to create shared adventures with newfound friends.

Navigating Customs – Embracing Local Traditions:

- Is This Acceptable? - Wach kayn chi mushkil?: Ensure that your actions align with local customs and traditions.
- How Do I Greet Properly? - Wach ghadi nsalim b lzwayj?: Seek guidance on proper greetings to show respect.

Embracing Serendipity – Going with the Flow:

- Let's See Where the Day Takes Us - Ghir nchoufou fin ghadi ykhdana: Embrace spontaneity and let the day unfold organically.
- Surprise Me - Khdni bissurat: Open yourself to delightful surprises and unexpected adventures.

Nature Appreciation – Communing with Marrakesh's Gardens:

- The Gardens Are Beautiful - Les jardins kaykouno jamilin: Revel in the beauty of Marrakesh's lush gardens and green spaces.
- I Feel at Peace Here - Kanmout b lkhir hna: Express the tranquility you experience in the midst of nature.

Fun Twist: Imagine yourself as a part of the garden's natural symphony – your presence adds a unique note to the melody.

Festival Fever – Immersing in Local Celebrations:

- What's the Best Festival to Attend? - Wach afdal lfestivals li nzour?: Seek recommendations for the most vibrant festivals to join.
- Tell Me Your Favorite Festival Memory - Goulili 3la ahsan dhikra dialk lifestival: Encourage locals to share their cherished festival experiences.

Musical Connections – Exploring Marrakesh's Melodies:

- Can You Recommend Traditional Music? - Wach ghadi tlba lik ala musiqa tradia?: Dive into the soulful tunes of Marrakesh with this inquiry.
- Let's Attend a Concert Together - Ghir nsawbo lmoussika m3a b3d: Invite fellow music enthusiasts to join you for a night of rhythmic joy.

Rooftop Revelry – Enjoying Panoramic Views:

- Where's the Best Rooftop View? - Fin ghadi ntlba afdal manzar mn lddakhl?: Discover elevated perspectives for breathtaking city views.

- I'm on Top of the World! - Ana f wssat lwelad!: Share the exhilaration of being atop Marrakesh with this enthusiastic phrase.

Sunset Serenity – Basking in Golden Horizons:

- Let's Watch the Sunset Together - Ghir nchoufou lghoroub m3a b3d: Share the magic of a Marrakeshi sunset with fellow admirers.
- This Sunset is Unforgettable - Had lghoroub kanmout b lzwayj: Capture the timeless beauty of the fading sun with this poetic expression.

MARRAKESH PRACTICAL TIPS AND ADVICE

SOUK SURVIVAL 101: Unleash Your Inner Bargainer

- Bargain like a pro, but make it a game. Channel your inner treasure hunter and remember, haggling is an art, not a battle.

TRANSPORTATION TANGO: Ride in Style

- Taxis are like magic carpets – negotiate your fare with flair. Think of it as a negotiation dance, and you might even get a friendly smile from your cabbie.

SPICE SAFARI: Savor the Flavors

- Dive into Moroccan cuisine, but watch out for the spice surprise. It's like a culinary adventure – one bite, and you're on a flavor rollercoaster.

MEDINA MAZE NAVIGATION: Get Lost with Purpose

- The Medina is a labyrinth, but think of it as your personal maze of wonders. Allow yourself to get lost, stumble upon hidden gems, and make every wrong turn an opportunity for discovery.

HAMMAM HINTS: Embrace the Steamy Experience

- Hammams are more than just baths; they're a cultural ritual. Imagine yourself as the protagonist in a Moroccan spa saga, with steam and relaxation as your allies.

RIAD RENDEZVOUS: Stay Like Royalty

- Choose a riad for your stay – it's not just accommodation; it's a chance to feel like Moroccan royalty. Pretend you're the ruler of your own mini palace.

JET-SETTING TO JEMAA EL-FNA: Nightly Spectacle Awaits

- Jemaa el-Fna is the heartbeat of Marrakesh. Treat it like your personal stage – enjoy the street performances, get lost in the music, and maybe, just maybe, join in the dance.

FASHION FORWARD IN THE SOUKS: Kaftans and Babouches Galore

- Souks are your fashion playground. Rock a kaftan like a runway model, slip into babouches with swagger, and strut through the market like you own it.

CULTURAL CODES: Respect and Revel in Traditions

- Respect local customs and traditions, but don't be afraid to ask questions. It's like a cultural exchange where everyone is a participant.

PHOTO PHENOMENON: Snap and Savor the Moments

- Capture moments, but don't forget to put the camera down and immerse yourself in the experience. Imagine every photo as a piece of your Marrakeshi story.

LEATHER LOVE AFFAIR: Bags, Belts, and More

- The leather goods are irresistible. Bargain with gusto and imagine each purchase as a stylish piece of Marrakesh that will travel with you.

CALL OF THE ADHAN: Let the Melody Guide Your Day

- Embrace the call to prayer – it's not just a sound; it's a melody that weaves through the fabric of the city. Let it be your daily anthem.

LANGUAGE LINGO: Salaam Aleikum and Shukran On Repeat

- Learn a few basic phrases – it's your linguistic passport to the soul of Marrakesh. Picture yourself as the charming linguist in a captivating dialogue.

TEMPLE OF TEA: Mint Tea Rituals

- Sip mint tea like it's a ceremony. Imagine each sip as a moment of serenity, a pause in the lively rhythm of the city.

HIGH-RISE SUNSET: Seek Rooftops for Golden Views

- Chase sunsets from a rooftop – it's not just a view; it's a golden spectacle. Picture yourself on a magical carpet, soaring towards the sun.

ARTISAN APPRECIATION: Handcrafted Treasures

- Dive into the souks like you're on a quest for hidden treasures. Every artisanal piece tells a story – imagine yourself as the hero unraveling these tales.

CONCLUSION

Dear Adventurous Soul,

As you reach the final pages of our whimsical guide, "Marrakesh Travel Guide 2024 Updated: Your Ultimate Guide to the Marvels and Mysteries of Morocco's Jewel City," let the echoes of Marrakesh linger in your heart like a cherished melody. We've embarked on a journey through the enchanting alleys, vibrant souks, and mesmerizing landscapes of this jewel city together, and what an adventure it has been!

In these pages, we've spun tales of spice-filled markets, soared over rooftops with the grace of a desert breeze, and navigated the labyrinthine medinas with the excitement of treasure hunters. Marrakesh has unveiled its marvels, from the lively chaos of Jemaa el-Fna to the serene beauty of Majorelle Gardens. We've danced through the nights, sipped mint tea in the afternoons, and embraced the rich tapestry of Moroccan culture.

As you close this guide, remember that Marrakesh is not just a city; it's a living story waiting for you to be its protagonist. Each phrase, tip, and piece of advice is an invitation to immerse yourself in the magic of this jewel city, to become a part of its tales, and to weave your own narrative amidst its marvels and mysteries.

To you, the intrepid explorer, we extend our heartfelt appreciation. Thank you for allowing us to be your travel companions, guiding you through the sweet chaos, the lively souks, and the tranquil gardens of Marrakesh. May your journey be filled with laughter, discovery, and the warmth of Moroccan hospitality.

As you step into the vibrant streets of Marrakesh, envision yourself as the lead in a grand adventure. Embrace the unexpected, savor the flavors, dance to the rhythm of the city, and let every moment be a chapter in the story of your Marrakeshi odyssey.

Here's to you, the storyteller of your own travel saga, and to the boundless wonders awaiting you in the heart of Morocco. Safe travels, adventurer, and may Marrakesh forever hold a special place in your wanderlust-filled heart.

With heartfelt gratitude,

Max Sterling

Printed in Great Britain
by Amazon

39221172R00056